To

A gift wrapped in my
prayers and best wishes

From

The Bedside
Book of
PRAYER

Contributing Writer
Gary Wilde

PUBLICATIONS INTERNATIONAL, LTD.

Louis Weber, C.E.O.
Publications International, Ltd.
7373 North Cicero Avenue
Lincolnwood, Illinois 60646

Permission is never granted for commercial purposes.

Manufactured in China.

8 7 6 5 4 3 2 1

ISBN: 0-7853-2169-1

The unattributed prayers in this book were written by Gary Wilde, a full-time freelance author and editor who has written numerous books, educational materials, and magazine articles on religious and self-help issues. One of his ongoing projects is editing the devotional quarterly *Quiet Hour*.

ONTENTS

OFFERING PRAISE AND THANKS

This is the day that the
LORD has made;
let us rejoice and be glad in it.

PSALM 118:24

OFFERING PRAISE AND THANKS

OFFERING PRAISE AND THANKS

I remember it—
coming from a swim
and lying back in white sand—
the gift of a moment to rest,
to sit in reverie,
to watch,
to close eyes and think of nothing
but the sound of breaking waves.
Yes, You were there with the sounds
and the sunshine,
and I am thankful.

OFFERING PRAISE AND THANKS

How good it is,
Almighty One,
to bask in the warmth of
your love.
To know nothing more
is required than this:
receive your good gifts
from above.

*B*e a gardener.
Dig a ditch, toil and sweat,
and turn the earth upside down
and seek the deepness
and water the plants in time.
Continue this labor
and make sweet floods to run
and noble and abundant fruits to spring.
Take this food and drink
and carry it to God
as your true worship.

JULIAN OF NORWICH (1332–1420)

OFFERING PRAISE AND THANKS

Water
that runs over moss-covered
rocks:
This is the sound of praise.
Fingers
that play upon ivory keys:
This is the sound of worship.
Silence
that speaks even better than
words:
This is the sound of my
thankful heart.

OFFERING PRAISE AND THANKS

OFFERING PRAISE AND THANKS

The steadfast love
of the LORD never ceases,
his mercies never come to
an end;
they are new every
morning;
great is your faithfulness.

LAMENTATIONS 3:22–23

OFFERING PRAISE AND THANKS

*L*ord,
since you exist, we exist.
Since you are beautiful, we are
beautiful.
Since you are good, we
are good.
By our existence we
honour you.
By our beauty we glorify you.
By our goodness we love you.

EDMUND OF ABINGDON
(1180–1240)

OFFERING PRAISE AND THANKS

OFFERING PRAISE AND THANKS

REACHING
OUT

*H*ere I am, Lord—
body, heart and soul.
Grant that with your love,
I may be big enough to reach
the world,
And small enough to be at
one with you.

COWORKER OF MOTHER TERESA

REACHING OUT

REACHING OUT

If I can throw a single
ray of light across the darkened
pathway of another;
if I can aid some soul to clearer
sight of life and duty,
and thus bless my brother;
if I can wipe from any human
cheek a tear,
I shall not have lived my life in
vain while here.

ANONYMOUS

REACHING OUT

REACHING OUT

Blessed be the God and Father
of our Lord Jesus Christ,
the Father of mercies and the God of
all consolation,
who consoles us in all our affliction,
so that we may be able to console those
who are in any affliction
with the consolation
with which we ourselves are consoled
by God.

THE APOSTLE PAUL,
2 CORINTHIANS 1:3–4

REACHING OUT

Across the room a smile
reached to me—
lifted my spirit.
Quick, bright,
it lit up my soul.
Who blessed me? I do not know.
I can only rehearse your sacred words,
and thrill at the prospect:

"Do not neglect to show hospitality to
strangers,
for by doing that some have entertained
angels
without knowing it."

REACHING OUT

REACHING OUT

*L*ord, open our eyes,
That we may see you in our
brothers and sisters.
Lord, open our ears,
That we may hear the cries of
the hungry, the cold,
the frightened, the oppressed.
Lord, open our hearts,
That we may love each other as
you love us.
Renew in us your spirit,
Lord, free us and make us one.

MOTHER TERESA (BORN 1910)

REACHING OUT

Knowing he
needs encouragement,
I pray for my friend,
Lord.
Lifting my heart to you
on his behalf,
may I not fail, either,
to reach my hand to his—
just as you are holding
mine.

REACHING OUT

REACHING OUT

26

God our healer,
whose mercy is like a
refining fire,
touch us with your judgment,
and confront us with your
tenderness;
that, being comforted by you,
we may reach out to a troubled
world,
through Jesus Christ.

JANET MORLEY

REACHING OUT

MOVING
THROUGH THE
STORMS

*Call on me in the
day of trouble;
I will deliver you,
and you shall glorify me.*

PSALM 50:15

MOVING THROUGH THE STORMS

MOVING THROUGH THE STORMS

God stir the soil,
Run the ploughshare deep,
Cut the furrows round and round,
Overturn the hard, dry ground,
Spare not strength nor toil,
Even though I weep.
In the loose, fresh mangled earth
Sow new seed.
Free of withered vine and weed
Bring fair flowers to birth.

PRAYER FROM SINGAPORE,
CHURCH MISSIONARY SOCIETY

MOVING THROUGH THE STORMS

MOVING THROUGH THE STORMS

I am still moving, God,
through storms.
By your grace—
over rough country,
you have carried me;
amidst pounding waves,
you have held me;
beyond the horizon of my longings
you have shown me your purposes.
Even in this small room, sitting still,
I am moving, God.
Closer.

MOVING THROUGH THE STORMS

When will the rain let
up, Lord?
Oh, soon:
may your presence
be to me as cleansing droplets
of mercy,
these clouds only filtering
in glorious gold and purple
the blazing rays of your grace.

MOVING THROUGH THE STORMS

MOVING THROUGH THE STORMS

*Even though I walk
through the darkest
valley,
I fear no evil;
for you are with me;
your rod and your staff—
they comfort me.*

PSALM 23:4

MOVING THROUGH THE STORMS

MOVING THROUGH THE STORMS

As storm clouds gathered, Father,
I used to run for cover,
panicked and picking a favorite escape.
None of them worked for long,
Dear God,
and none of them kept me safe.
No more running then.
I see it clearly now:
Wherever I am standing
is a special place,
under the shadow of your
sheltering wing.

MOVING THROUGH THE STORMS

SEEKING COURAGE

The things, good Lord, that we pray for, give us the grace to labour for.

ST. THOMAS MORE (1478–1535)

SEEKING COURAGE

SEEKING COURAGE

Our Father in heaven,
hallowed be your name.
Your kingdom come.
Your will be done,
on earth as it is in heaven.
Give us this day our daily bread.
And forgive us our debts,
as we also have forgiven our debtors.
And do not bring us to the time of trial,
but rescue us from the evil one.

JESUS, MATTHEW 6:9–13

SEEKING COURAGE

SEEKING COURAGE

44

*Y*ou call me to courage,
Lord,
but incrementally,
as a child emboldened
to walk along
placing each small foot in
larger footprints.
Following Father or Mother—
as I am following you—
knowing a path marked out
this way—just step by step—
by you
can only lead to safety.

SEEKING COURAGE

*B*lessed are the poor in spirit,
for theirs is the kingdom of heaven.
Blessed are those who mourn,
for they will be comforted.
Blessed are the meek,
for they will inherit the earth.
Blessed are those who hunger and thirst
for righteousness,
for they will be filled.
Blessed are the merciful,

SEEKING COURAGE

for they will receive mercy.
Blessed are the pure in heart,
for they will see God.
Blessed are the peacemakers,
for they will be called children of God.
Blessed are those who are persecuted for
righteousness' sake,
for theirs is the kingdom of heaven.

JESUS, MATTHEW 5:3–10

SEEKING COURAGE

I am
feeling my way
in this darkness, God,
and it seems I'm going in circles.
Yet you have reminded me
—quietly, just now—
that encircled by your love
with every move in any direction
I go no closer to you
—nor farther either—
than already centered
I am.

SEEKING COURAGE

SEEKING COURAGE

SEEKING COURAGE

*S*eeking courage, Lord,
I bundle my fears
and place them in your hands.

Too heavy for me,
too weighty even to ponder
in this moment,

such shadowy terrors
shrink to size in my mind
and—how wonderful!—
whither to nothing in your
grasp.

SEEKING COURAGE

FINDING
PEACE

Grant, O Lord,
that we may live in thy fear,
die in thy favour, rest in thy
peace, rise in thy power, reign
in thy glory.

WILLIAM LAUD (1573–1645)

FINDING PEACE

FINDING PEACE

*I*n silence
I kneel in your presence—
bow my heart
to your wisdom;
lift my hands
for your mercy.
And open my soul to the
great gift:
I am already held
in your arms.

FINDING PEACE

The LORD bless you
and keep you;
the LORD make his face to
shine upon you,
and be gracious to you;
the LORD lift up his
countenance upon you,
and give you peace.

NUMBERS 6:24–26

FINDING PEACE

I didn't think it possible,
in a crowd, to be
touched
jostled
elbowed into
your peace, Lord.
It makes me smile to recognize your
suffusing
invading
pursuing presence,
calling, cajoling:
a delicate whisper
overwhelming
even this noise.

FINDING PEACE

FINDING PEACE

Do not worry about
anything,
but in everything by prayer and
supplication
with thanksgiving
let your requests be made
known to God.
And the peace of God,
which surpasses all
understanding,
will guard your hearts and your
minds.

PHILIPPIANS 4:6–7

FINDING PEACE

PRAYERS OF THE HEART

*H*e prayeth best who
loveth best
All things both great and small;
For the dear God who loveth us,
He made and loveth all.

SAMUEL TAYLOR COLERIDGE (1772–1834)

PRAYERS OF THE HEART

*I*t's hard, Lord, to reveal my heart
to you,
though it's the thing I most want to do.
Remind me in this dialogue
that you already know what is within me.
You wait—O thank you!—hoping
for the gift of my willingness
to acknowledge
the good you already see
and the bad you've long forgotten.

PRAYERS OF THE HEART

PRAYERS OF THE HEART

*L*ord, grant me a
simple, kind, open,
believing,
loving and generous
heart,
worthy of being your
dwelling place.

JOHN SERGIEFF (1829–1908)

PRAYERS OF THE HEART

PRAYERS OF THE HEART

You listen
as a hearer of my heart.
And this is a moment to
remind myself:
Prayers have never
needed words.

*M*y soul yearns for
you in the night,
my spirit within me earnestly
seeks you.
For when your judgments are
in the earth,
the inhabitants of the world
learn righteousness.

ISAIAH 26:9

PRAYERS OF THE HEART

68

PRAYERS OF THE HEART

In every waking moment,
it seems,
my heart stretches
for this one thing—
searching faces for it,
reaching hands for it,
lifting prayers for it.
Yes, for the one thing
which—remind me, again and again!—
is.
Simply is.
Here.
Always:
Your love.

PRAYERS OF THE HEART

ACKNOWLEDGMENTS

The publisher gratefully acknowledges the kind permission granted to reprint the following copyrighted material. Should any copyright holder have been inadvertently omitted, they should apply to the publisher, who will be pleased to credit them in full in any subsequent editions.

Meditations With Julian of Norwich, by Brendan Doyle, © 1983, Bear & Co., Santa Fe, New Mexico, used with permission.

Silence of the Heart: Meditations by Mother Teresa of Calcutta, compiled by Kathryn Spink, published by SPCK © 1985, used by permission of the publishers.

All Desires Known, by Janet Morley © 1988, used by permission of Morehouse Publishing, Harrisburg, Pennsylvania.

"Prayer from Singapore" used with permission from the Church Missionary Society.

My Life in Christ, by John Sergieff, translated by E.E. Gowaeff, published by Holy Trinity Monastery, used with permission by Holy Trinity Monastery.

ACKNOWLEDGMENTS *(continued)*

The Scripture quotations contained herein are from the *New Revised Standard Version* of The Bible, © 1989 by the Division of Christian Education of the National Council of the Churches of Christ in the United States of America, and are used by permission. All rights reserved.

PHOTO CREDITS

Front cover: "Sunrise, Brent at Low Water," by Julian Novorol. Private collection, The Bridgeman Art Library. Used with permission.

FPG International: Willard Clay: 63; Richard H. Johnston: 53, 69; E. Nagele: 5, 41; Barbara Peacock: 54; Thayer Syme: 61; Telegraph Colour Library: 23; Renaud Thomas: 12; Ron Thomas: title page, 18, 36; **International Stock:** Peter Langone: 17; Ron Sanford: 6; **Superstock:** 15, 30, 32, 35, 38, 42, 49, 58, 64, 66, 71; Christie's, London: 20, 44, 50; Musée du Louvre, Paris: 11; National Gallery, Oslo, Norway: 26; Vatican Museums & Galleries, Rome: 29.